# Why Bosses Don't Hustle

## "7 Steps to a more Unified Command"

I0441237

Ryan Amamoo

ISBN:

# DEDICATION

I dedicate this book to my family, who all played parts in building the man I am today.

# CONTENTS

# 1 VISION

" A OG is one who Stands on his own feet, A BOSS is ONE who Guarantees that WE gon' eat" –RICK ROSS

Welcome to our book on how to go from an overworked hustler to an organized business owner. As a self-made entrepreneur, I share my personal journey of discovering the true value within myself when I recognized the hustler's spirit coursing through my veins. Hustling tirelessly in various endeavors to make ends meet, I realized that while impressive, my list of hustles led to burnout and costly mistakes. I learned that there's a significant difference between hustling and scaling a business.

In our book, I aim to shed light on the distinction between being a hustler and becoming a boss. As I reflect on my own experiences, I want to guide aspiring entrepreneurs away from the path of endless hustling and towards building a successful and sustainable business.

I recount my younger years spent juggling full-time jobs, engaging in various ventures like selling drugs, creating music,videos for local artists, promoting clubs, and doing wedding photography. While these hustles provided temporary solutions to financial challenges, they lacked the long-term vision needed for true success.

On my journey into the realm of entrepreneurship, I can trace the genesis of my hustler mentality back to my high school days, where the rhythmic beats of lunchtime freestyle sessions ignited a spark within me. As I sat at the table, surrounded by peers channeling their creative energy through rhythmic beats and spontaneous rhymes, I realized the potential for something greater.

The lunchtime gatherings often transformed into impromptu rap battles, drawing in a captivated audience. It was in those moments that I recognized a unique opportunity to blend my passion for music with a budding entrepreneurial spirit. This was the inception of my side business.

Seizing the spotlight, I introduced an array of products to the hungry crowd. Burnt CDs, meticulously curated playlists of the latest hits and underground tracks, became a sought-after commodity. Alongside the music, I offered premium snacks to satiate the appetites of those entranced by the beats and verses. But my entrepreneurial endeavors didn't stop there; I ventured into the world of bootleg movies, including some of the more risqué selections, attuned to the diverse tastes of my audience.

As I navigated this unconventional marketplace, I learned the art of identifying opportunities within seemingly ordinary moments. The lunchtime rap battles were not just a creative outlet but also a stage for me to showcase my entrepreneurial prowess. It taught me the importance of adaptability, understanding my audience, and capitalizing on unexpected circumstances.

This chapter of my life became a foundational experience, shaping the hustler within me. It instilled the belief that success can emerge from the fusion of passion and keen observation, turning everyday occurrences into lucrative ventures. The journey was only beginning, but the lessons learned during those lunchtime sessions laid the groundwork for a mindset that would guide me through future challenges and opportunities.

However, every story of growth and self-discovery encounters its share of challenges, and mine was no exception. In the midst of one of the rap battles, the tone shifted unexpectedly when a fellow rapper decided to use my appearance and clothing as fodder for his rhymes. Despite the personal nature of the jabs, I had reached a point in my journey where I could detach from such comments and view them as opportunities for growth rather than personal attacks.

In that moment, instead of letting the words sting, I saw an opportunity to demonstrate resilience and creativity. Drawing from the reservoir of experiences that had shaped me thus far, I crafted a response in the form of a surprise rhyme. The tables turned as I skillfully interwoven humor, wit, and a sharp sense of self-awareness into my verses. The unexpected twist not only diffuse the tension but also garnered admiration from the onlooking crowd.

This episode became a pivotal moment in my journey, teaching me the power of resilience and the ability to transform adversity into an opportunity for personal triumph. It reinforced the idea that challenges, even when directed at the core of one's identity, can be reframed and used as stepping stones toward personal growth.

The positive outcome served as a testament to the strength derived from self-assurance and creativity in the face of adversity. It became clear that maintaining a strong sense of self, coupled with the ability to navigate challenges with grace and wit, was an indispensable aspect of the hustler's mindset.

This experience, along with the countless others woven into my narrative, further fueled my evolution as an entrepreneur and instilled a deep understanding that true resilience lies not in avoiding challenges, but in transforming them into opportunities for self-expression and advancement.

Eager to carve a unique path in the world of music, my entrepreneurial spirit led me to a new venture—creating and selling my own music. Joining forces with my friend A.D, we birthed the musical entity known as Kamp Life.A.D. and Sotru Nestled in the vibrant city of Huntsville, Alabama, our artistic endeavors soon gained traction and resonated with the local community.

In our pursuit of musical excellence, the hustle took on a new dimension. Beyond the rhythmic beats and soulful lyrics, we ventured into the realm of entrepreneurship once again. Car Washes became more than just a means to keep our vehicles spotless; they became a source of income to fund our musical aspirations. T-shirts adorned with the Kamp Life brand became not only a fashion statement but a tangible representation of our passion and dedication. Every sale propelled us further on our musical journey.

The hustle extended beyond merchandise and carwashes; it became a constant companion in our pursuit of excellence.

Studio time and new equipment weren't handed to us; we earned them through relentless determination and an unwavering commitment to our craft. The power of hustling lay not only in the financial gains but in the invaluable lessons learned along the way.

This period of my life taught me the art of resourcefulness and the importance of perseverance. Every carwash, every t-shirt sold, and every product moved brought us one step closer to our dreams. The hustle wasn't just about financial gain; it was a mindset that propelled us forward, pushing the boundaries of what we thought was possible.

Through Kamp Life, I discovered that the true power of hustling lies in the relentless pursuit of one's passions, coupled with a willingness to adapt and innovate. It became a transformative journey where each entrepreneurial endeavor, no matter how small, contributed to our collective growth. The hustle was not just a means to an end; it was a philosophy that became ingrained in our approach to life, music, and success.

For these reasons I hold utmost respect for those who demonstrate a strong work ethic and tenacity, commonly referred to as "hustlers." In my perspective, the concept of hustle transcends mere activity; rather, it embodies a state of mind that drives individuals to achieve their goals. Similarly, being a boss entails a consistent commitment to excellence and productivity.

It is essential to clarify that my intentions are not to denigrate hustlers in any way. Instead, I seek to draw a comparison between the mindset of a hustler and that of a boss. Both have valuable roles in the world, and I genuinely appreciate the contributions of hustlers. In fact, I actively seek partnerships with like-minded individuals who possess this enterprising spirit.

During my hustle years as a fence installer, a significant turning point emerged when I secured a contract with a local roofing company. This collaboration materialized as they dealt with damaged roofs resulting from storms, and they entrusted me with subcontracting the fence work. Although the relationship experienced its share of challenges, it blossomed into a longstanding and fruitful business partnership.
Amid this journey, I forged a close friendship with one of the esteemed salesmen, whom I will refer to as RJ. RJ impressed me with his exceptional salesmanship and his genuine qualities as an individual. He was deeply rooted in his religious beliefs, attending church regularly, and exhibited an unwavering love for people, consistently displaying a willingness to lend a helping hand. I observed RJ's remarkable

growth as he built his own company from the ground up, each step deliberate and guided by a clear vision.

Throughout his tenure at the previous company, RJ often voiced concerns about operational and procedural aspects. However, he wisely formed alliances with other skilled salesmen, collaborating on major projects and generously sharing his commissions with them. It was through RJ's recommendations that I was connected with these esteemed salesmen, ultimately leading to the establishment of my first LLC.

An incident arose where RJ was not duly compensated for his contributions to a substantial commercial project. Unable to reach a satisfactory resolution with his former employer, RJ amicably parted ways and made the decision to initiate his own roofing company, all the while maintaining a positive relationship with his previous boss. Remarkably, every salesman and subcontractor who had worked directly with RJ faithfully followed him to his new venture, including myself. Reflecting back, it became evident that RJ had already exemplified the traits of a true leader from the day he started his role. His journey displayed various boss moves, as outlined below:

Vision: harbored a clear and unwavering vision of becoming an owner.

Leadership and Foundation: He anchored his leadership approach in his religious beliefs, providing a strong and authentic foundation for his endeavors.

Financial Management: exhibited relentless dedication to sales, ensuring effective financial management.

Strategic Planning: He was vocal about recognizing and refining company procedures for the benefit of customers.

Networking: fostered meaningful connections and friendships with other accomplished salesmen and subcontractors.

Delegation: Recognizing the need to lighten his workload while building his company, he delegated responsibilities and involved other salesmen in larger projects, strategically paving the way for his brand's growth.

RJ's journey stands as a testament to his entrepreneurial acumen and the embodiment of a true boss, inspiring and guiding those around him to follow in his path of success.

I wanted to share his story because I feel it can be applied to by anyone who is looking to scale or break the hamster wheel of overworking.

As you may have noticed I refer to this book as our book. So no it was not a typo lol. My Vision is for you to use this book as a journal in building what you want and the plan to get it with the mindset of a successful business owner. So I shared my vision for our book and Rj's Vision for his business. I included some space Below for you to write your vision. Remember in the words of multi-billionaire

Aliko Dangote
"Always be Intentional about the words you speak"

1.Vision:_____

_____

_____

_____

The core objective of our book is to guide and  understand the critical difference between a hustler and a boss. A hustler may make significant money, but their time and energy are continuously consumed by day-to-day operations. On the other hand, a boss scales their business strategically, automating services, and building a reliable team to handle operations while they focus on growth and development.

The journey from hustler to boss is not just about making more money; it's about achieving freedom and fulfillment.With that being said I will offer practical insights on the list below

Defining Hustler and Boss: I start by clearly defining the characteristics of a hustler and what sets them apart from a boss. This understanding lays the foundation for transformation.

Recognizing Burnout and Mistakes: We will identify and tag the signs of burnout and understand the costly mistakes that come with hustling without a long-term vision.

Embracing a Scaling Mindset: I provide strategies to assist with the transition from a hustler's mindset to that of a boss, focusing on scalability, automation, and building a sustainable boss routine.

Building a Reliable Team: To succeed as a boss, we will navigate the importance of assembling a trustworthy and capable team to share the workload and contribute to the company's growth.

I want our book to serve as a valuable resource for those seeking to create a thriving business that can function even when they're not personally handling every task. Ultimately, it's about achieving success while reclaiming one's time, freedom, and sense of purpose.

## 2 LEADERSHIP

Leadership Excellence: The Cornerstone of Business Success

Leadership is the guiding force behind every successful business. It's the art of inspiring and influencing individuals to achieve a common goal. In this exploration, we'll dive deep into the world of leadership, dissecting its core principles, and understanding its significance in the business landscape. Drawing inspiration from various leadership icons and their journey through the realms of hip-hop, we'll unravel the secrets to leadership excellence and its pivotal role in shaping successful enterprises.You might have already noticed the deliberate structure in commencing each chapter with a well-defined plan and then faithfully executing it. This deliberate approach isn't by chance; it's a reflection of a leadership principle that's absolutely essential. As a leader, one of your most vital tasks is to nurture not only plans for your team but also for yourself.

## Leadership Defined

Leadership is not merely a position or a title; it's a way of being and a set of actions. As the late Nipsey Hussle put it, "I'm about seeing long-term, seeing a vision, understanding nothing really worthwhile happens overnight, and just sticking to your script long enough to make something real happen." True leadership involves vision, perseverance, and a commitment to making things happen in the long run.

In the business world, leaders are individuals who set the direction, inspire their teams, and drive organizational success. They possess the ability to motivate others, make tough decisions, and navigate through challenges with resilience.

## Leading by Example

Leadership begins with setting an example. Just as in religion where Pastors like Bishop T.D. Jakes lead by example through his sermons and business  deals, leaders must walk the talk. Leading by example means embodying the values, work ethic, and integrity you expect from your team.So  proper delegating behind the scenes cultivates the hustle spirit  throughout the workspace.

When your team sees you consistently demonstrating dedication, honesty, and a strong work ethic, they are more likely to follow suit. In the words of J-Cole, "I'm Ahead of my time like I live my whole life backwards"." Leaders should instill a culture of continuous vision and commitment.

## Vision and Strategy

A clear vision is the North Star that guides leaders and their organizations. Leaders, like Dr. Dre when he envisioned his record label Aftermath Entertainment, must articulate a compelling vision that inspires and motivates their teams. A well-defined vision provides direction and purpose, aligning the efforts of everyone within the organization.

Effective leaders complement their vision with a sound strategy. Strategy involves a systematic approach to achieving goals, much like how Nas meticulously crafts his lyrics. Leaders must create strategic plans that outline the steps needed to turn their vision into reality.

## Communication and Collaboration

Effective leadership hinges on communication and collaboration. Leaders need to communicate their vision, goals, and expectations clearly and consistently. Just as in the world of hip-hop, where collaborations between artists often produce groundbreaking music, collaboration in business leads to innovation and success.

Leaders should foster an environment where open communication and collaboration are encouraged. This includes actively listening to team members, valuing diverse perspectives, and leveraging the collective intelligence of the organization.

## Adaptability and Resilience

Adaptability is a hallmark of great leaders. The business landscape is constantly evolving, much like the ever-changing beats in hip-hop. Leaders must be flexible and open to change, adjusting their strategies as needed to navigate through challenges and seize opportunities.

Resilience is another essential trait. As 50 Cent once said, "I'm not afraid to die. I'm afraid not to try." Leaders face setbacks and adversity, but their ability to bounce back, learn from failures, and persevere sets them apart. Resilience is the anchor that keeps leaders steadfast in turbulent times.

## Empowerment and Trust

Leadership is not about micromanagement; it's about empowering others. Like a record producer empowering artists to create their best work, leaders should trust their teams to excel. Empowerment fosters a sense of ownership and accountability among team members.

Trust is the foundation of empowerment. Leaders must trust their team's capabilities and judgment. When trust is present, individuals feel valued, motivated, and empowered to take initiative, make decisions, and contribute their best efforts.

## Emotional Intelligence

Emotional intelligence (EQ) is a vital component of effective leadership. It involves recognizing and managing one's emotions and understanding and influencing the emotions of others. EQ enables leaders to navigate complex interpersonal dynamics with finesse.

Artists like Kanye West channel their emotions into their music. Similarly, leaders should harness their emotional intelligence to build strong relationships, empathize with team members, and inspire trust and collaboration.

## Decision-Making and Accountability

Leaders are responsible for making critical decisions that impact the organization's direction and success. These decisions can be as game-changing as choosing the next hit single Effective decision-making requires gathering information, analyzing options, and considering the consequences.

Accountability is the flip side of leadership. Leaders must hold themselves and their teams accountable for their actions and outcomes. They set high standards and ensure that individuals take ownership of their responsibilities.

## Diversity and Inclusion

Inclusion is the cornerstone of effective leadership in today's diverse business landscape. Just as hip-hop thrives on a diverse array of voices and perspectives,

Commencing this chapter, my aim is to elucidate the very essence of being a leader. The intention is to cultivate a mental environment that seamlessly embodies these principles in real-time. True leadership, I believe, is akin to casting a stone into a tranquil body of water, where the ripples of your actions extend far beyond the initial point of impact. Once your strategic plan is set into motion, the art lies in being poised to act promptly and delegate responsibilities judiciously.

In this orchestration of leadership, a crucial component is the establishment of an empowered team. While positive thinking is a widely advocated principle, I propose that, as leaders, we shoulder the responsibility of contemplating potential challenges with a realistic lens. This pragmatic approach not only allows you to anticipate potential project issues but also ensures a proactive stance.

However, it's imperative to note that dwelling on potential negatives should not become a descent into the abyss of despair. Rather, consider it a navigational tool for your journey. Many dreams have succumbed to the fear of failure, yet I find solace in this very place. For, in my perspective, it is far more advantageous to confront and learn from failure in the rehearsal phase than to encounter it on the grand stage of accomplishment. In the realm of leadership, embracing a realist mindset becomes a compass guiding you through the intricacies of challenges and, ultimately, towards the championship of your aspirations.

Reflecting on a pivotal experience, there was a time when a client expressed dissatisfaction with the progress of a project, particularly in obtaining the necessary permit. This was a new client, eager to have the doors open within a stringent 60-day deadline from the project's commencement. In my optimism, I assured the client that the ambitious timeline could be met.

However, as the project unfolded, unforeseen challenges emerged, compelling an extension of the timeline by an additional 5 months. Understandably, frustration ensued, and the client insisted that no invoices would be settled until the permit was secured. To exacerbate the situation, work had already been executed, and my subcontractors were awaiting compensation. As a small business owner, the prospect of informing my team at week's end that their payments were delayed was a distressing thought. As a leader, I faced a series of tough decisions, all within a tight 24-hour window.

Firstly, I had to strategize on how to persuade the client to honor their financial commitment. Simultaneously, I needed to devise a contingency plan to ensure my team received their due payments promptly. Additionally, resolving the issues with the city to secure the elusive building permit became a critical priority. Most importantly, I recognized the need for a profound change in approach to prevent finding myself in a similar predicament in the future.

This transformative moment compelled me to reassess and fortify my leadership strategies. The lessons learned paved the way for a more resilient and proactive mindset, ensuring that the intricate dance of project management, client expectations, and financial responsibilities would harmonize seamlessly in the future. It underscored the importance of strategic foresight, adaptability, and continuous improvement in navigating the challenges inherent in small business ownership.

Immersed in this challenging scenario, I dedicated hours of intense focus, grappling with self-inflicted mental turmoil for not identifying the issues earlier and establishing the right expectations. The irony stung – the pertinent information lay freely available on the city's website, a resource I neglected to explore. As time dwindled with no apparent solution in sight, I chose to step back. I indulged in self-care, playing video games and opting for an early bedtime. In the quiet hours of 4:30 am, a strategic plan descended upon me like a revelation.

Compelled by this newfound clarity, I meticulously crafted a comprehensive job summary, detailing the completed tasks and the journey that led us to this critical juncture. Acknowledging that changes initiated by the customer were a catalyst for the issues, I took ownership of my oversight regarding city regulations, a key factor impacting the project timeline. Armed with this insight, I presented the client with a transparent update encompassing a revised timeline, budget, and a fresh action plan capable of reducing the completion time by two months.

Convening an emergency meeting onsite while our team was diligently at work, I shared my findings with the client. From a position of strength, I demonstrated accountability for my role in the situation. Remarkably, the continued visible progress despite prior uncertainties rebuilt the client's confidence in our capabilities. Despite earlier reservations, the client agreed to settle outstanding payments to subcontractors and greenlit the project to proceed.

This transformative experience highlighted the potency of resilience, strategic thinking, and accountable leadership. It underscored the significance of adapting to unforeseen challenges, learning from missteps, and, most importantly, demonstrating a commitment to transparency and resolution. In navigating the intricacies of project management, this episode became a compass guiding me towards an enhanced understanding of effective leadership in the face of adversity.

Leadership is truly a key quality and should be at the forefront of your frequent education in becoming a better business owner.By placing leadership at the forefront of your ongoing education as a business owner, you invest in the very foundation that shapes the trajectory of your venture. It's not just about managing operations; it's about inspiring, influencing, and creating a lasting impact on both your business and those you lead. Continuous refinement of your leadership skills is an investment that pays dividends in the sustainable growth and success of your enterprise.

## 3 Art of Adaptability

In the fast-paced world of business, the terms "boss" and "hustler" are often used to describe individuals who navigate the entrepreneurial landscape. While both these roles have their place in the business world, the skill of adaptability emerges as a key factor in determining long-term success. This article explores why bosses need the skill of adaptability to run a business effectively, without downplaying the importance of hustling. Drawing inspiration from the world of hip-hop, which has produced some of the most successful entrepreneurs, we'll examine how adaptability can be the difference-maker for bosses.

The Hip-Hop Hustle: A Powerful Force

Hip-hop culture has always been associated with hustling. From the streets of the Bronx to global stages, hip-hop artists have embodied the spirit of entrepreneurship. Jay-Z, often referred to as "Hova" in the hip-hop world, has exemplified the art of hustling. His lyrics and business ventures illustrate how hustling can lead to immense success: "I'm not a businessman; I'm a business, man." This mantra encapsulates the essence of the hip-hop hustle, where artists leverage their talents into empires.

Indeed, hustling is a valuable tool for business owners. It encompasses determination, relentless effort, and the drive to achieve one's goals. In the world of hip-hop, artists like Jay-Z, Dr. Dre, and Diddy have parlayed their musical careers into lucrative businesses spanning fashion, technology, and entertainment. Their relentless pursuit of success, often rooted in humble beginnings, has inspired generations.

However, it's essential to recognize that hustling, while indispensable in its own right, can be one-dimensional. The pure hustle mindset often focuses on short-term gains, immediate results, and sometimes involves cutting corners. In contrast, adaptability provides a broader perspective, offering a strategic advantage for long-term success in running a business.

Adaptability: The Unsung Hero

Adaptability is the skill of being able to adjust to new conditions and circumstances. It involves a willingness to learn, evolve, and pivot in response to changing markets, technologies, and consumer preferences. While hustling can help you seize opportunities, adaptability ensures your business remains relevant and resilient over time.

In hip-hop, there are numerous examples of artists who started with one style and adapted to new trends, staying relevant across generations. Eminem, for instance, initially gained fame with his raw, controversial lyrics, but he didn't rest on his laurels. He adapted his music and approach to stay relevant as the industry changed. His versatility allowed him to endure and thrive, even as new artists emerged.

Similarly, in business, adaptability is a vital trait for bosses. The corporate landscape is continually evolving, with technological advancements, economic shifts, and consumer behavior changes. Companies that fail to adapt risk becoming obsolete. A classic example of adaptability in business is Netflix. What began as a DVD rental service evolved into a streaming giant, continually adjusting its strategy to meet consumer demands.

So Why do Bosses Need Adaptability?Here are 4 good reasons below:

1. Navigating Uncertainty:
   In business, uncertainty is a constant. Economic downturns, unexpected crises, and industry disruptions can happen at any time. Bosses who possess adaptability can pivot quickly and find new opportunities within the chaos. This skill enables them to steer their businesses through turbulent waters and emerge stronger on the other side.

   Hip-hop artist Nas once said, "Life's a b***h, and then you die." The sentiment applies to business as well. Unpredictable challenges will arise, and adaptability is the lifeline that helps bosses persevere.

2. Staying Relevant:
   Just as hip-hop artists need to stay relevant in an ever-changing music landscape, businesses must remain up-to-date in their respective industries. The ability to adapt to evolving trends and technologies is crucial for survival.

   Consider Apple, which started as a computer company and later shifted its focus to consumer electronics, introducing game-changing products like the iPhone. This adaptability allowed Apple to maintain its position as a global tech giant.

3. Embracing Innovation:

The world of hip-hop thrives on innovation, with artists pushing the boundaries of music, fashion, and culture. In the business world, innovation is equally vital. Bosses who prioritize adaptability are more likely to embrace new ideas, technologies, and strategies that can lead to growth and innovation.

Amazon's founder, Jeff Bezos, exemplifies this. He started as an online bookstore but adapted to become a global e-commerce giant, introducing innovations like Prime membership and Amazon Web Services.

4. Building Resilience:

Adaptability is closely linked to resilience. Bosses who are adaptable are better equipped to bounce back from setbacks and failures. They view challenges as opportunities for growth rather than insurmountable obstacles.

As hip-hop icon Tupac Shakur once said, "I don't have no fear of death. My only fear is coming back reincarnated." In the business world, adaptability allows bosses to transform challenges into stepping stones toward success.

While hustling remains a powerful tool for business owners and is exemplified in the world of hip-hop, adaptability emerges as the unsung hero that bosses need to better run their businesses. The fast-paced, ever-changing landscape of business demands the ability to pivot, innovate, and navigate uncertainty.

In the words of hip-hop legend Biggie Smalls, "Stay far from timid; only make moves when your heart's in it, and live the phrase 'sky's the limit.'" Bosses can embrace the hustle mentality to make bold moves, but they should combine it with adaptability to ensure their businesses not only survive but thrive in the long run.

In the end, it's not a matter of downplaying hustling but recognizing that adaptability is the secret weapon that can elevate a boss from short-term success to lasting impact in the business world, much like hip-hop legends who have transcended time and trends through their ability to adapt and evolve. So, whether you're in the recording studio or the boardroom, remember that adaptability is the key to staying on top in the game.

## 4 Financial Mastery

In the world of business, the roles of "bosses" and "hustlers" often intertwine, both striving for success and recognition. In the world of finance and business management, the term "boss" carries a unique significance. It represents a position of leadership, responsibility, and strategic decision-makingWhile hustling represents an undeniable force of determination and drive, financial management emerges as a vital skill that bosses need to run a business effectively. In our book, we explore the idea that financial management is more about thoughtful strategy and less about frantic hustle. Let us delve into why bosses require financial management skills and why they shouldn't discredit the value of hustling. Drawing inspiration from the world of hip-hop, which has produced both successful entrepreneurs and hustlers, we will examine how financial management can be the cornerstone of long-term business success while acknowledging the power of hustling.

Hip-hop culture has always celebrated the hustle—a relentless pursuit of success against all odds. Artists like Jay-Z, who started from humble beginnings, embody the hustle mentality. Jay-Z's lyrics reflect the ethos of hustling, "I'm not a businessman; I'm a business man."

Hustling is, indeed, a valuable tool for business owners. It encompasses qualities like perseverance, resilience, and the drive to achieve goals against adversity. The lessons from hip-hop's hustlers, who rose from adversity to build empires, serve as a testament to the power of hustle in the business world.

As Warren Buffett once said, "The stock market is designed to transfer money from the Active to the Patient." This perspective underscores the importance of a patient, strategic approach to financial management that aligns with the goals of the boss.

Warren Buffett's quote, "The stock market is designed to transfer money from the Active to the Patient," encapsulates a profound insight into the world of investing and financial management. Let's delve deeper into the meaning and implications of this quote and how it underscores the importance of a patient and strategic approach to financial management, aligning with the goals of the boss.

## 1. Understanding the Stock Market Dynamics:

The stock market is a dynamic and complex entity where millions of investors engage in buying and selling securities like stocks, bonds, and mutual funds. Prices of these assets fluctuate daily based on a multitude of factors, including economic indicators, corporate performance, geopolitical events, and investor sentiment.

## 2. The Active Investor's Approach:

Active investors are those who frequently buy and sell stocks, often attempting to capitalize on short-term price fluctuations. They may engage in day trading, momentum trading, or speculative strategies. These investors aim to make quick profits by taking advantage of market volatility.

## 3. The Passive Investor's Approach:

On the other hand, passive investors adopt a more patient and long-term perspective. They focus on strategies like buy-and-hold, index investing, and dividend reinvestment. Passive investors are less concerned with short-term market fluctuations and more focused on the fundamental strength of their investments.

## 4. Patient Strategic Approach:

Buffett's quote suggests that the stock market tends to reward patient investors over the long term. This perspective aligns with the goals of the boss, who is often more interested in building sustainable wealth and achieving long-term financial success rather than engaging in high-frequency trading for quick gains.

## 5. The Importance of Patience:

In the stock market, prices can be highly unpredictable in the short term. Market sentiment, news events, and speculation can lead to rapid price movements that may be unrelated to a company's underlying value. Patient investors, however, are less swayed by short-term market noise. They remain focused on the intrinsic value of their investments and are willing to weather the ups and downs of the market.

## 6. The Power of Compounding:

One of the critical advantages of a patient approach to financial management is the power of compounding. When you invest for the long term and reinvest dividends or interest, your wealth can grow exponentially over time. This compounding effect can significantly enhance your overall returns, making it a powerful tool for building wealth.

## 7. Reducing Transaction Costs and Taxes:

Frequent trading, which is common among active investors, can lead to higher transaction costs, such as brokerage fees and taxes on short-term capital gains. In contrast, patient investors who minimize buying and selling can reduce these costs, allowing more of their capital to stay invested and grow over time.

## 8. Embracing Informed Decision-Making:

A patient and strategic approach to financial management encourages informed decision-making. Bosses who prioritize patience are more likely to conduct thorough research, analyze financial statements, and consider the long-term prospects of their investments. This diligence can lead to more sound investment choices.

## 9. Overcoming Emotional Biases:

Emotions can play a significant role in investment decisions. Active investors often succumb to fear and greed, leading to impulsive actions. In contrast, patient investors are better equipped to overcome emotional biases and make rational choices based on their long-term objectives.

## 10. Achieving Financial Goals:

Ultimately, the patient and strategic approach to financial management aligns with the boss's broader financial goals. Whether the goal is retirement planning, wealth preservation, or building a financial legacy, a patient strategy is more likely to lead to success.

In conclusion, Warren Buffett's quote underscores the value of patience and a strategic approach to financial management. It suggests that the stock market is not a place for rapid wealth accumulation through frenetic trading but rather a platform where sustainable wealth is built over time. The boss, guided by this wisdom, is more likely to navigate the complexities of the financial world successfully, aligning their actions with their long-term objectives and ultimately achieving financial mastery.

Understanding stock market investments is not only relevant to personal financial management but also plays a crucial role in business financial management. Here's how the knowledge and principles related to stock market investments can be applied to business financial management:

In the world of financial management, it's like we've got two distinct tracks to run on – the "Active Investment" track, akin to the street hustle, and the "Passive Approach" track, more aligned with a strategic financial strategy. When I applied these tracks to my construction business, I'll admit, the initial results were far from impressive. I found myself questioning if I'd made a wrong move, caught in the hustle's fast lane. That's when I decided to pump the brakes, take a break, and focus on less taxing work. Little did I know, this decision was the ultimate chess move.

In the words of Biggie Smalls, "Stay far from timid, only make moves when your heart's in it." So, I took a step back, let my long-term strategies marinate, and gave them the space and time they needed to flourish. Slowly but surely, what was once a sluggish start became a consistent, reliable income stream. I realized that sometimes, in the world of finance, "Slow and steady wins the race," as they say.

This newfound approach not only provided financial stability but also gave my mind and body the much-needed relief from the high-stress hustle. I had more time to breathe, to reflect, and to refine my business strategies. It was like Jay-Z said, "I'm not a businessman; I'm a business, man." And a successful business knows how to evolve and thrive.

So, my advice to you is simple – take another look at those 10 steps above, just like you'd spin a classic hip-hop vinyl, and craft your very own financial management plan. Because in the world of finance, just like in hip-hop, it's not just about the beats; it's about the rhythm, the flow, and the strategy that sets you up for long-term success.

1._____

_____

2._____

_____

3._____

_____

4._____

_____

5._____

_____

6._____

_____

7._____

_____

8._____

_____

9._____

_____

10._____

_____

Knowledge is power but without action it's dead so be sure to keep the above commitmentment to yourself just how you show up and show out for your customers.

In the hip-hop world, financial management is akin to a well-crafted verse—it requires precision and strategy. Just as artists like Kendrick Lamar meticulously craft their lyrics, business owners must meticulously manage their finances.

One of the key differences between hustling and financial management is the focus on long-term vision. The hustler may seize immediate opportunities, but the boss employs financial management to ensure those opportunities align with a broader, sustainable strategy.

As Nas also rhymed, "I need a new n***a for this black cloud to follow." In the business world, bosses need to look beyond the immediate clouds and consider the long-term forecast. Financial management provides the roadmap to navigate through both sunny and stormy days.

One of the ultimate goals for many business owners is to leave behind a lasting legacy and generational wealth. Hustling can accumulate wealth, but financial management ensures the preservation and growth of that wealth for future generations.

In the words of hip-hop mogul Diddy, "I'm not in it for the money. I'm in it for the love." Bosses who employ financial management skills are driven not just by money but by the love for their businesses and the desire to leave a lasting financial legacy.

In the world of business, the hustle is a powerful tool that can lead to short-term success and open doors. However, as our exploration has shown, bosses who prioritize financial management are better equipped to build sustainable, resilient, and enduring businesses.

As hip-hop has taught us, both the hustle and financial management have their places in the entrepreneurial journey. The key is to strike a balance, harnessing the power of hustle to seize opportunities while leveraging financial management to ensure long-term success. In doing so, bosses can create a harmonious symphony of ambition and strategy, ultimately achieving financial mastery.

5 Customer Focus

## The Heartbeat of Business Success

At the heart of every thriving business is an unwavering commitment to customer focus. It's a philosophy that places customers at the center of every decision, action, and innovation. In this exploration, we'll delve into the world of customer focus, unraveling its core principles, and unveiling its paramount importance in the business realm. Drawing inspiration from various industries and leaders who have mastered the art of putting customers first, we'll illuminate the path to creating enduring customer-centric enterprises.
In the year 2023, the landscape of the hip-hop world is undeniably characterized by themes revolving around drugs, sex, wealth, and the allure of a criminal lifestyle associated with hustling. When I speak of "Boss's Don't Hustle," it's easy to understand why the average person might assume I'm referring to this particular form of hustling, and they wouldn't be entirely wrong. However, it's crucial to recognize that while

this aspect of hustling is certainly part of the picture, it's far from the whole story.

Fortunately, I'm not here to engage in debates about what's right or wrong, or to delve into conspiracy theories about Illuminati mind control. As my wise grandmother used to say, "I don't have a hell to throw you into, or a heaven to kick you out of," which reminds us that it's not my place to pass judgment on others.

Instead, my focus is directed toward exploring the intriguing connections that exist between street hustling and the activities of everyday business owners. Specifically, I'm interested in the realm of Customer Focus, where these seemingly disparate worlds can intersect and share valuable lessons.

In this exploration, we'll delve into how the principles of effective customer engagement, relationship-building, and adaptability, which are often second nature to street hustlers, can be applied by entrepreneurs and business professionals to enhance their customer-oriented strategies. By drawing parallels between these two seemingly distinct worlds, we can unearth valuable insights and learn how to create exceptional customer experiences that resonate across all domains, from the urban streets to the corporate boardrooms.

w you in, or a heaven to kick you out of" so it is not my place to judge you. .

## Customer Focus Defined

Customer focus is more than a business strategy; it's a mindset that prioritizes the needs, preferences, and experiences of customers. It's about creating value for clients and forging lasting connections. In a world where customers have a multitude of choices, businesses that excel in customer focus set themselves apart.

## The Customer-Centric Culture

Building a customer-centric culture is the bedrock of customer focus. It means instilling a shared belief within the organization that the customer is paramount. As business magnate Richard Branson once said, "Clients do not come first. Employees come first. If you take care of your employees, they will take care of the clients."

This culture encourages employees to actively seek ways to enhance customer satisfaction. It promotes empathy, active listening, and a genuine desire to exceed customer expectations.

## Customer-Centric Strategy

A customer-centric strategy involves aligning all business activities with customer needs and desires. It's not about offering what the company thinks customers want, but about truly understanding their preferences. As Amazon's Jeff Bezos notes, "We see our customers as invited guests to a party, and we are the hosts. It's our job every day to make every important aspect of the customer experience a little bit better."

This strategy guides product development, marketing, sales, and customer service, ensuring that every aspect of the business caters to customer demands.

## Listening to the Voice of the Customer

Listening to the voice of the customer is akin to tuning in to their desires, concerns, and feedback. This process involves actively seeking and incorporating customer input into decision-making. As Sam Walton, the founder of Walmart, emphasized, "There is only one boss. The customer. And he can fire everybody in the company from the chairman on down, simply by spending his money somewhere else."

Businesses use various tools and techniques, such as surveys, focus groups, and social media monitoring, to capture the voice of the customer and adapt their strategies accordingly.

## Personalization and Customization

In a world of mass production, personalization and customization are the keys to winning customer loyalty. These approaches allow businesses to tailor products, services, and experiences to individual customer preferences. As Steve Jobs famously stated, "You've got to start with the customer experience and work back toward the technology, not the other way around."

By offering personalized recommendations, custom-made products, and tailored services, businesses create memorable and unique experiences for their customers.

## Continuous Improvement

Customer focus is an ongoing commitment to improvement. It involves constantly seeking ways to enhance the customer experience and deliver more value. As the management guru Peter Drucker said, "Quality in a service or product is not what you put into it. It is what the customer gets out of it."

Businesses employ techniques like Six Sigma, Lean principles, and Kaizen to identify areas for improvement and eliminate inefficiencies, ensuring that customers consistently receive the best.

## Building Customer Trust

Trust is the cornerstone of customer relationships. Businesses must be reliable, transparent, and consistent in their interactions. As Warren Buffett aptly noted, "It takes 20 years to build a reputation and five minutes to ruin it. If you think about that, you'll do things differently."

By consistently delivering on promises, addressing concerns promptly, and maintaining open communication, businesses build and maintain customer trust.

## Loyalty and Advocacy

A customer-focused approach leads to customer loyalty and advocacy. Loyal customers not only return for repeat purchases but also become brand advocates who recommend the business to others. As Shep Hyken, a renowned customer service expert, suggests, "Customer service is not a department. It's a philosophy."

Businesses that prioritize customer focus cultivate strong, long-lasting relationships with customers who become ambassadors for their brand.

## The Competitive Edge

Customer focus isn't just a philosophy; it's a competitive advantage. Companies that consistently provide exceptional customer experiences outperform their competitors. As business magnate Bill Gates observed, "Your most unhappy customers are your greatest source of learning."

By learning from customer feedback and continuously evolving to meet their needs, businesses gain a significant edge in the marketplace.

## Conclusion

In the grand tapestry of business success, customer focus stands as a vibrant thread that weaves through every aspect of an organization. It's a commitment to putting customers at the forefront, listening to their needs, and exceeding their expectations. Just as a skilled artisan crafts a masterpiece, businesses that prioritize customer focus create enduring relationships, loyalty, and a legacy of success.

In the lyrical tapestry of my friend A.D's words, particularly the poignant lines from the song "Gangsta" in the album "Kamp Life Legends," a profound perspective on life and career objectives emerged. "My Career Objectives is to get money and hustle, under special skills put surviving and bussing." These words, once perceived as a mere reflection of our younger days, now serve as a profound segue into the next chapter of my journey — the chapter on resilience.

A.D's lyrics, with their raw authenticity and unapologetic commitment to the hustle, reveal a deeper wisdom and foresight. What might have seemed like a simple declaration of ambition in our youth now unfolds as an early manifestation of the skills essential for a true businessman. The emphasis on "surviving and bussing" echoes the fundamental components of resilience — the ability to navigate challenges, adapt to circumstances, and emerge stronger.

As I reflect on those lyrics, I recognize that resilience is not just about weathering the storms of life; it's about thriving in the face of adversity. A.D's words serve as a testament to the resilience embedded in our very aspirations. The pursuit of financial success and the relentless hustle are not merely ends in themselves; they are a manifestation of a resilient mindset, a commitment to overcome obstacles, and an unwavering determination to achieve our goals.

In the broader context of our journey, these lyrics become a beacon guiding us through the challenges inherent in the pursuit of success. The early signs of wisdom and vision within those lines lay the foundation for the resilience that would become a defining characteristic of our entrepreneurial endeavors.

The next chapter in this self-help narrative delves into the concept of resilience — exploring its facets, understanding its significance, and drawing lessons from the experiences that shaped my journey. It's a journey where the seemingly straightforward lyrics of a song become a profound source of inspiration, illuminating the path towards a resilient and prosperous future.

## 6  Resilience

"Don't try to fit a square peg into a round circle/
That $#!T will hurt you" – Nas
I get frustrated with myself when I don't succeed in business.
However, facing challenges and setbacks in business can be
disheartening, but it's important not to be too hard on yourself.
Failure is a natural part of the entrepreneurial journey, and
many successful business owners have experienced multiple
failures before achieving their goals. I used to hear things like
that , and my first thought would be 'Bulshit ". They had some
lucky break or talent that I don't have that thrust them into
success. Right! Surely that is way they are doing better than
me, Right? Wrong, the simple answers are the hardest to
accept when they are about us. The Truth is, by leaning into
my own understanding that my problems are unique to this
world, hindered me from dealing with early errors in the
beginning. These little errors turned into fatal habits later in my
hustle years. All the failures I have endured I see now as
master classes on what not to do . So all the quotes I hear
now about failure being life lessons I  take those opportunities
to check myself, business and personal.

No Matter the problem. Here are some steps you can consider taking to improve your situation:

**Learn from Failures:** Instead of dwelling on past failures, try to understand the reasons behind them. Identify what went wrong and what you could have done differently. Use these experiences as learning opportunities to make better decisions in the future.

**Seek Support and Guidance:** Consider finding a mentor, joining a business networking group, or seeking advice from experienced entrepreneurs. Learning from others who have faced similar challenges can provide valuable insights and support.

**Create a Solid Business Plan:** Outline a clear and comprehensive business plan for your future ventures. Include realistic financial projections, marketing strategies, and an analysis of potential risks and opportunities.

*Practice recognizing when you need to ask better questions

**Work on Financial Management:** Improve your financial literacy and money management skills. Create a budget to track your expenses, explore ways to increase your income, and work on repairing your credit.

**Consider a Small Scale Start:** Instead of diving into a large business venture, start small and test your ideas on a smaller scale. This approach can help you minimize risks while gaining valuable experience.

Embracing the wisdom of the small-scale start was a pivotal move in my journey, one I now recognize as the epitome of strategic brilliance. As my construction business evolved, its complexity outpaced my own skill set. Specializing as a fence contractor, I found myself inundated with homeowners seeking comprehensive projects. Eager to accommodate, I'd dive in, employing subcontractors for tasks beyond my personal expertise – a venture that carried a daunting 50/50 risk of success or failure.

Recognizing the gamble, I made a conscious decision to pivot away from larger undertakings. My focus shifted towards the intricacies of smaller repairs: fixing leaning gates, addressing damaged fence sections, and replacing posts. The impact was profound; not only could I command higher prices for these specialized services, but I could also complete them swiftly and seamlessly. Stepping back from the grandiose allowed me to mitigate risks and optimize profits.

This transformative experience isn't confined to construction; its principles resonate across diverse business landscapes. The key takeaway echoes the age-old adage – sometimes, less truly is more. By recalibrating your approach and honing in on the essentials, you, too, can minimize risks and enhance your bottom line, irrespective of your industry. It's a paradigm shift that has the potential to redefine your success story.

A great habit to develop in unsure times are to refresh your vision and ask yourself ,

**What is a Successful Business Owner?**_____

_____

_____

_____

Uncertain times serve as a crucible for unveiling our resilience, reminiscent of the wisdom shared by Young Jeezy: "Look up in the sky and tell me what you see, the clouds, Nah homie not me. I see opportunity, I'm an opportunist" from the track "Sky's the Limit" in the album "Let's Get It: TM 101." This lyric resonates deeply with me because it encapsulates a profound truth. The challenges and adversities we face are undeniably real; adopting a simplistic "think positive" approach often feels inadequate when we're grappling with the lows of life. In those moments, positivity might be the last thing on our minds, and it's entirely okay.

During periods of anger or frustration, I advocate for acknowledging those emotions without letting them dictate your actions. Rather than succumbing to the immediate impulse to react, consider engaging in activities completely unrelated to the source of your distress. Much like the elusive nature of forgotten names that suddenly resurface when you least expect it, tackling complex problems can benefit from a mental reset.

In my perspective, approaching challenging situations with a mindset detached from the immediate turmoil often yields clearer, more objective, and logical thinking. It's akin to dispelling brain fog. So, as you navigate through uncertainties, grant yourself the space to experience and process negative emotions. Then, redirect your focus towards activities you enjoy. In doing so, you may find that the fog lifts, unveiling a clearer path to confront challenges with resilience and a more composed state of mind.

As an entrepreneur, I've come to recognize that a significant portion of business challenges revolves around financial matters. In these critical junctures, I intentionally dial down my emotions and refocus on the core vision and dream that propelled me to become a successful business owner. My aim is to encourage you to adopt a similar practice, employing it as a powerful reset mechanism to anchor yourself in your purpose.

This self-check is pivotal not only for honoring the commitments you make to others but, more importantly, for staying true to your own aspirations and cultivating your personal character. In the realm of business, authenticity begins with being honest with oneself.

A prosperous business owner embodies a myriad of qualities, skills, and attributes crucial for the sustained growth of their enterprise. While this may sound ideal, the reality is that none of these qualities can flourish without adept financial management skills. Whether you acquire these skills personally or enlist the expertise of a professional, such as a freelancer well-versed in tools like QuickBooks, is up to you.

The beauty is that trustworthy freelancers abound, both online and locally. If the idea of entrusting a stranger doesn't sit well with you, leverage your network. Tap into the wisdom of your friends and acquaintances; seek recommendations and align yourself with someone who shares your values. Remember, building a successful business requires not only strategic vision but also a solid foundation of financial acumen. Trust the process, and align yourself with the right financial support to ensure the growth and longevity of your entrepreneurial journey.

Here are some key factors that make a successful business owner:

**Vision:** A successful business owner has a clear vision of what they want to achieve with their business. They have a long-term plan and set ambitious yet achievable goals to guide their decision-making.

**Leadership:** Effective leadership is crucial for managing employees, inspiring teams, and driving the business forward. A successful business owner leads by example, fosters a positive work culture, and empowers employees to perform at their best.

**Adaptability:** Markets and industries are constantly evolving, and a successful business owner must be able to adapt to changing circumstances and seize new opportunities. Flexibility and openness to innovation are essential traits.

**Financial Management:** Strong financial management skills are vital to a business owner's success. They should be able to manage cash flow, budget effectively, and make informed financial decisions.

**Customer Focus:** Understanding and meeting customer needs are paramount in any successful business. A successful business owner prioritizes customer satisfaction, listens to feedback, and continually strives to improve their products or services.

**Resilience:** The path to success is rarely smooth, and setbacks and challenges are inevitable. A successful business owner remains resilient, perseveres through tough times, and learns from failures.

**Networking:** Building and maintaining strong relationships within the industry and the business community can lead to valuable partnerships, collaborations, and opportunities.

**Marketing and Sales:** Knowing how to effectively market products or services and close sales is crucial for growth. A successful business owner understands their target market and employs effective marketing strategies.

**Delegation:** A successful business owner recognizes that they can't do everything themselves and delegates tasks to capable team members. This allows them to focus on strategic decisions and higher-level responsibilities.

**Continuous Learning:** The business landscape is constantly changing, and successful business owners are always eager to learn and stay updated with industry trends, new technologies, and best practices.

**Integrity and Ethics:** Trust is essential in business, and a successful business owner operates with honesty, transparency, and ethical practices. This fosters trust among customers, employees, and partners.

**Time Management:** With numerous responsibilities, a successful business owner must manage their time efficiently and prioritize tasks to make the best use of their resources.

**Passion and Determination:** Successful business owners are passionate about what they do, and their determination drives them to overcome obstacles and achieve their goals.

It's important to note that success in business is not solely determined by these factors, and different industries and ventures may require additional specific skills and expertise. Additionally, success is not a static achievement; it requires continuous effort, adaptation, and improvement.

In the realm of self-discovery and empowerment, even after the crucial act of resetting and clearing the mind, challenges may persist. However, true mastery of resilience transcends mere intellectual understanding; it necessitates the fusion of knowledge with decisive action. Setbacks, rejections, and failures often prey on our confidence and self-worth, leaving us depleted. The sole remedy lies in taking deliberate steps forward.

Consider this process as akin to a baby's journey in learning to walk. The initial crawl symbolizes the foundational step, and if life's hurdles knock you down, it's perfectly fine if you can't immediately spring back to your feet. What matters is the commitment to keep crawling toward your aspirations until you gather the strength to sprint towards them.

This progression is a testament to the resilience within, a journey where every intentional movement, no matter how small, contributes to your eventual triumph. By embodying this principle, you not only weather the storms of adversity but also emerge stronger, more assured, and fully aligned with the unstoppable force of your own potential.

Overcoming hard times and seemingly unsolvable problems can be a challenging but ultimately rewarding process. Here are some steps to guide you through:

1. **Acceptance and Acknowledgment:**

   - Acknowledge the difficulty of the situation and accept that challenges are a part of life.

   - Recognize your emotions and allow yourself to feel them without judgment.

2. **Break It Down:**

- Divide the problem into smaller, more manageable parts.

- Tackle each component separately, focusing on practical steps rather than feeling overwhelmed by the entirety.

3. **Seek Support:**

   - Reach out to friends, family, or a mentor for emotional support and perspective.

   - Sharing your struggles can provide valuable insights and alternate viewpoints.

4. **Develop a Positive Mindset:**

   - Cultivate a positive outlook by focusing on what you can control.

   - Challenge negative thoughts and replace them with affirmations or constructive statements.

5. **Explore Solutions:**

   - Brainstorm potential solutions without judgment initially. Let creativity flow.

   - Evaluate each solution critically, considering the pros and cons.

6. **Learn and Adapt:**

- View challenges as opportunities for growth and learning.

- Adaptability is key; be willing to modify your approach based on what works and what doesn't.

7. **Set Realistic Goals:**

- Establish achievable short-term goals that contribute to solving the larger issue.

- Celebrate small victories along the way to maintain motivation.

8. **Self-Care:**

- Prioritize self-care to maintain physical and mental well-being.

- Ensure you get adequate rest, exercise, and engage in activities that bring you joy.

9. **Professional Help:**

- If the problem persists, consider seeking professional help, whether it's counseling, coaching, or consulting experts in the field.

10. **Maintain Perspective:**

   - Put the challenge in perspective by considering the bigger picture of your life.

   - Remember past difficulties you've overcome and the strength you gained from those experiences.

11. **Practice Patience:**

   - Solutions may take time to unfold. Practice patience and stay committed to the process.

12. **Celebrate Progress:**

   - Acknowledge and celebrate the progress you make, no matter how small.

   - Grounded  reinforcement boosts morale and reinforces your ability to overcome challenges.

You might have observed a deliberate repetition in some of the steps discussed, and I assure you, this repetition is intentional. Embracing the essence of the Rule of 7, it is essential to understand that a prospective individual needs to encounter a message at least seven times before taking the decisive action of investing in a product or service. This principle holds a profound truth that extends beyond marketing – it echoes in the corridors of personal development.

As your companion on this transformative journey towards success, my plea is not merely for you to passively consume these words. Instead, I implore you to infuse them into the very fabric of your everyday life. The Rule of 7 becomes your guide, urging you to internalize, reflect, and, most importantly, act upon the wisdom imparted.

Remember, reaching out for assistance is not a sign of weakness, and challenges are an inevitable facet of the human experience. By approaching these challenges armed with resilience, adaptability, and a firmly grounded mindset, you not only navigate through the storms of adversity but also pave the way for innovative solutions to seemingly insurmountable problems. In embodying these principles, you embark on a journey of personal growth, where intentional repetition becomes the key to unlocking the doors of lasting transformation and unparalleled success.

## 7 Networking

"Total networking
Last chance to advance and stash grands
If you have plans to have fam and mad land"--Rakim

"Let's kick off this chapter with a new perspective on networking. Often, when we think of networking, our minds conjure images of elegant soirées, where the art of engaging in small talk weaves the tapestry of fascinating stories. These interactions, though sometimes peppered with clichés, hold a unique charm and allure. But before you cringe at the familiarity of it all, rest assured there's a point to these tales.

Networking, you see, is like the symphony of a grand social event. Each conversation, like a musical note, contributes to the overall melody of your professional journey. So, in the pages that follow, we'll explore how these seemingly ordinary encounters can be the key to unlocking extraordinary opportunities in the world of business."

It's hardly a secret that my passion for music extends beyond just hip-hop. Classical and rock music have always held a special place in my heart as well. Whether it's immersing myself in the soothing melodies of classical tunes or grooving to African house beats, I often turn to music, particularly before challenging meetings or as a backdrop during prolonged hours on the computer.

In drawing parallels between music and networking, I've chosen to use musical instruments as a metaphor. The essence lies in the art of assembling the right sounds, just as success in networking hinges on connecting with the right partners. Just as a symphony composed of harmonious elements produces the best music, forging alliances with the right partners yields optimal results for customers. This, in turn, contributes to building a successful reputation, where customers willingly pay for services, confident in the delivered outcomes.

Please don't be too harsh in judging as you read the forthcoming short story—I assure you, it serves a purpose. (lol)

Title: The Unseen Symphony - A Tale of Collaborative Greatness

Once upon a time, in the bustling city of Prospera, there lived a group of enterprising individuals, each a hustler in their own right. Meet Alex, the visionary artist with a paintbrush that could breathe life into mere canvases. Then there was Max, the tech-savvy wizard, whose fingers danced effortlessly on keyboards, conjuring digital wonders. Sarah, the master communicator, possessed a silver tongue that weaved stories with mesmerizing grace. And finally, there was Chris, the financial virtuoso, whose magic with numbers could turn pennies into fortunes.

Individually, they marveled at the rhythm of their daily pursuits, working tirelessly to achieve their dreams. Yet, despite their remarkable talents, they found themselves facing struggles unique to their paths. Alex's beautiful artwork couldn't find the right audience, while Max's brilliant inventions lacked exposure. Sarah's eloquent words often fell on deaf ears, and Chris struggled to secure the financial backing needed for his ambitious ventures.

One fateful day, fate wove its magic, and these hustlers found themselves drawn together by an inexplicable force. As if guided by an unseen hand, they crossed paths, sharing their stories of triumphs and tribulations. The spark of collaboration ignited, and a newfound understanding dawned upon them - the power of unity.

Each brought their unique instrument to the ensemble, recognizing that their collective talents complemented one another. Alex's vivid imagination fused seamlessly with Max's digital prowess, giving birth to immersive experiences that captivated audiences. Sarah's eloquent narratives gave life to the visions of Alex and Max, while Chris' financial acumen transformed their dreams into tangible realities.

Their collaboration flourished like a flourishing garden, with each member nurturing the other's growth. The struggles that once weighed heavily on their shoulders now became shared burdens, lightened by the strength of unity. They faced challenges with unwavering support, knowing that their symphony's true beauty lay in harmony.

As their collaborative masterpiece took shape, it spread its wings beyond Prospera, reaching the ears of other hustlers in search of something greater. The spirit of collaboration spread like wildfire, as more like-minded souls joined their ensemble. Together, they formed an orchestra of visionary brilliance, transforming the city into a thriving ecosystem of collaborative greatness.

Yet, as with any great symphony, there were moments of discord. Egos clashed, visions diverged, and tempers flared. But the hustlers of Prospera knew that the true magic lay in embracing their differences and forging a common path. They learned to harmonize their ambitions, each finding their unique role in the symphony of collaborative greatness.

As they embraced collaboration's beauty, their shared purpose ignited an unyielding bond. They no longer saw each other as rivals but as comrades on a shared journey. They celebrated one another's victories, rejoicing in the knowledge that their strength lay in unity.

In the heart of Prospera, their harmonious symphony echoed far and wide, leaving an indelible mark on the world. The collaborative brilliance of Alex, Max, Sarah, and Chris transformed the city's landscape, elevating it to unprecedented heights of innovation and prosperity.

Their achievements multiplied beyond imagination, achieving more together than they ever could alone. As they basked in the beauty of collaborative greatness, they realized that true wealth was not solely measured by riches, but by the profound fulfillment of shared purpose.

And so, dear reader, remember the tale of Prospera, where hustlers became a symphony of collaborative greatness. As you turn the pages of your own life's story, may you find the magic that lies in unity, and may your collaborative journey lead you to a crescendo of everlasting success and fulfillment.

In the story of Alex, Max, Sarah, and Chris, we see how a network of like-minded business owners can be a powerful source of support when you're facing challenges or pursuing ambitious goals. Here are a few key lessons we can draw from their experience:

**1. Diverse Skillsets:** Each member of this group brought unique skills and talents to the table. Alex's creativity, Max's digital expertise, Sarah's storytelling ability, and Chris's financial acumen created a well-rounded team. When business owners collaborate with others who possess complementary skills, they can overcome obstacles and seize opportunities more effectively.

**2. Creative Synergy:** The fusion of Alex's imagination with Max's digital skills resulted in immersive experiences that captivated audiences. This collaboration demonstrates that when like-minded individuals come together, their collective creativity can lead to innovative solutions and products that might not be possible individually.

**3. Amplifying Vision:** Sarah's eloquent narratives gave life to the visions of Alex and Max. Sometimes, sharing your vision with fellow business owners who understand your goals can help you clarify your ideas and bring them to life. A network of like-minded individuals can serve as a sounding board and offer constructive feedback to help you refine your concepts.

**4. Financial Guidance:** Chris's financial acumen played a crucial role in transforming their dreams into tangible realities. Business owners often face financial challenges, and having a network of peers who can offer advice, share their experiences, or even collaborate on financial matters can be invaluable.

**5. The Power of Unity**: The story illustrates that these entrepreneurs, despite their differences, united around a common goal. The power of unity and shared objectives can be a driving force in overcoming challenges, whether they are related to competition, market changes, or personal setbacks.

In the realm of networking, intentionality is your compass. When you're pitching ideas to potential partners, it's not just about a transaction; it's about crafting a compelling narrative that illustrates the mutual benefits without disrupting their existing routines. Equally crucial is to offer a clear exit strategy, a graceful conclusion, in case plans don't align. The ultimate aim? To nurture and sustain robust, meaningful business relationships.

The individuals who stand as my friends today are those with whom I've weathered challenges, and those with whom I've ventured into profitable endeavors – sometimes, the fortunate ones are those where both elements converge.

Consider this: In the world of business, it's not merely a matter of what you know, but more often, it's who you know. Your contact list is a goldmine of untapped opportunities waiting to be transformed into low-cost business ventures. And in your quest to cultivate these connections, remember that the art of storytelling and providing clear, graceful exits can be your most potent tools.

So, here is my challenge for this chapter. Leverage your existing relationships, building partnerships, and exploring cost-effective business opportunities. Cellphone contact list try letting the right people know about your business offer a discount or a weekend special. The same can and should be done on social media. You never who needs your service or product right now.Because, as the adage goes,  "Your network is your net worth"

Who needs my
service/product?_____

Who do I know that Works with these kinds of
people?_____

What Value can you offer to others in
return?_____

Are there other business owners that share a common
problem?

_____

Is there something you can create or offer that will solve the
problem
?_____

Are there any local events or clubs you can join for your given
industry?_____

I posed these pivotal questions to you not merely for contemplation but because they guided me toward a transformative idea that significantly altered my personal trajectory. In my journey as a contractor, I encountered a common struggle pervasive among fellow contractors in my locale—difficulties in crafting accurate estimates and navigating the often labyrinthine process of obtaining permits for substantial projects. Rather than succumb to the challenges, I chose to convert this adversity into an opportunity for growth.

Harnessing the power of innovation, I conceived a product specifically designed to address the very pain points that afflicted contractors like myself. This strategic move not only alleviated my own challenges but also presented a valuable solution to a wider audience of professionals in the same predicament. By creating a tangible and marketable solution, I not only transformed my personal circumstances but also established a business model that allowed me to empower and assist others facing similar hurdles.

The essence of this transformative journey lies in the realization that challenges, when approached with a solution-oriented mindset, can be transformed into stepping stones toward personal and professional success. In your own endeavors, consider the challenges you face not as roadblocks but as opportunities to innovate, create, and ultimately propel yourself toward a brighter future.

In the process of conversing with app developers about my innovative solution, I received a surprising suggestion: the product had potential not only among fellow contractors but also among homeowners seeking streamlined solutions. This unforeseen insight opened up new horizons and prompted me to explore the untapped market of homeowners grappling with similar challenges.

To enhance the accessibility and user-friendliness of the product, I recognized the need for instructional videos. Initially, this aspect seemed like a potential hindrance, but as I delved deeper, I discovered an unexpected avenue for expansion. The creation of instructional videos not only served as a valuable tool for users but also transformed into an auxiliary service with significant potential.

Realizing the dual purpose of these videos, I seized the opportunity to position them as a lead service. The instructional content became not just a guide for utilizing the product effectively but also a gateway to additional offerings. This revelation sparked an innovative approach: I packaged the videos and product as a comprehensive online course tailored for aspiring entrepreneurs venturing into the realm of construction sales.

By aligning the product with educational content, I not only enhanced its market appeal but also established a new revenue stream. This diversification not only catered to the needs of homeowners but also extended a helping hand to budding entrepreneurs seeking guidance in the complex landscape of construction sales. In essence, what initially seemed like a setback evolved into a strategic move that broadened the scope of my venture and fostered growth beyond the initial target audience.

Diving headlong into this transformative concept required a substantial investment on my part, but the rewards were nothing short of remarkable—I successfully cultivated three distinct streams of income. The journey, however, was far from a smooth sail; there were numerous moments when the weight of the endeavor threatened to overwhelm me, and thoughts of quitting loomed ominously.

In those challenging times, I became my own best advocate, heeding the very advice I had imparted to others. Recognizing the significance of seeking guidance from seasoned professionals, I reached out to mentors and experts in the field. Their insights not only provided a roadmap for navigating the intricacies of my entrepreneurial venture but also served as a source of motivation during moments of doubt.

Persisting through the hurdles, I ultimately brought the product to fruition, turning it into a lucrative source of income. The financial gains not only validated the effort invested but also afforded me the luxury of reclaiming some precious personal time. This newfound freedom became a catalyst for pursuing another passion—writing this very book.

The arduous yet rewarding journey underscores a crucial lesson: perseverance, coupled with strategic guidance, can transform ambitious ideas into tangible success. As you embark on your own ventures, remember that challenges are inherent in the entrepreneurial path, but with determination and a willingness to seek wisdom from those who have trodden similar paths, you can overcome obstacles and unlock the potential for multiple streams of income.

In the pursuit of realizing my innovative app idea, I made a strategic decision to double down on a specific niche—fence repair work. This deliberate focus served a dual purpose: not only did it ensure a steady and consistent income, but it also afforded me the financial stability to invest significantly in the development of my app. This intentional concentration on fence repair work became a cornerstone in the foundation of my entrepreneurial journey.

Simultaneously, I recognized the immense value of networking in the business landscape. Engaging with fellow contractors became more than just a means of expanding professional connections; it evolved into a vital strategy for introducing my app to a broader audience. Through networking, I not only sustained my fence repair business but also forged connections with other contractors who, much like myself, could benefit from the innovative solution I was developing.

This confluence of strategic focus and networking proved to be a dynamic combination, propelling my entrepreneurial endeavors to new heights. The lesson here is clear: networking is not just a casual aspect of business; it is a potent tool that can catapult you towards your goals. Whether you aspire to be a boss leading a team of hustlers or a visionary entrepreneur, the relationships you build through networking can be the catalyst that propels you to your desired destination. Embrace the power of connections; it might be the key to elevating your status from a hustler to a successful Boss.

Embedded within the rhythmic verses of my personal lyrics, penned 14 years ago, lies a declaration that encapsulates the evolution of my journey. "Now I'm Riding Clean, Hustling, Focusing on Commas/ Had a conference with my CEO's bout to execute this Come up," as voiced by SoTru in the album "Kamp Life Legends," echoes the transformative power of resilience and ambition.

In these lyrics, the transition from riding clean and hustling to a focus on commas symbolizes a progression not just in financial status but in mindset. The hustler's journey is not static; it is a dynamic process of growth and elevation. The reference to a conference with CEOs signifies a shift towards leadership and strategic thinking — a trajectory that unfolds as a natural consequence of relentless hustle and unwavering resilience.

Reflecting on these words now, I can't help but smile at the audacity of my younger self, unaware of the magnitude of the path I was paving. The reference to becoming a CEO was more than a mere aspiration; it was a declaration of intent, a commitment to ascending the ranks of entrepreneurship. Little did I know then that the journey toward becoming a CEO would be filled with challenges, triumphs, and a continual process of learning.

As I share this personal lyric, my hope is that it serves as a testament to the potential for growth and transformation embedded in each of us. The realization of my role as a CEO, a position that once seemed aspirational, is now a source of pride. It stands as a testament to the resilience, adaptability, and entrepreneurial spirit that have become integral to my identity.

In concluding this chapter of our book, I extend the same aspirations to you, the reader. May the lessons and insights shared here empower you on your unique journey. As I laugh at the boldness of my yonger self, I also acknowledge the growth, wisdom, and strength gained along the way. May this book be a guide, a source of inspiration, and a companion as you navigate the hustle of your own life, executing the come-up you envision.

# ABOUT THE AUTHOR

As an aspiring author, I've embarked on a remarkable journey filled with learning and creativity. My passion for storytelling traces its roots back to my childhood, where I would craft stories and poems to share with friends while building treehouses and creek rafts. Over the years, my writing evolved into hip hop storytelling, an avenue for me to express my creativity.

The book, "Why Bosses Don't Hustle," is a reflection of my own experiences in the everyday grind. I've learned that trying to do it all on my own was not only overwhelming but also detrimental to my well-being and financial stability. The journey of writing this book has been a testament to the importance of delegation and teamwork.

In the future, I'm excited to channel my creative energy into the realm of science fiction novels, exploring new horizons and imaginative landscapes. I invite you to stay tuned for Part 2 of this series, where I'll delve into the transformation from street hustling to efficient business delegation. Thank you for joining me on this journey, and I hope my experiences and insights have resonated with you.

www.ingramcontent.com/pod-product-compliance
Lightning Source LLC
Chambersburg PA
CBHW022344290526
45786CB00014B/2473